# Con

## To the Student

Read with your teacher

Learning to spell and read new words is fun. It is exciting to learn how our language is made up of sounds and fun to put these sounds together in different patterns. Learning all the sounds we use in the English language will help your spelling and reading. Do you know, for example, the different ways to spell the sounds of *o*? Just plain *o* is not the only way: *o*-consonant-*e* says /ō/ as in *home, oa* says /ō/ as in *boat, oe* says /ō/ as in *toe,* and *ow* says /ō/ as in *snow.* It really is very easy to learn these sounds when you learn a few at a time.

## To the Teacher

Words, phrases, and sentences for dictation are found in our manual, *How to Teach Spelling.* Sentences (in boldface type) that tell the students to write material from dictation have footnotes that tell the teacher which pages in *How to Teach Spelling* contain the material to be dictated. Dictate only as much material as you think your students can handle at one time. Usually it is best to dictate a few words, a few phrases, and a few sentences until all have been given. If students need more practice, you may repeat any of the material.

Answers to the exercises are in a separate key.

Laura Toby Rudginsky
Elizabeth C. Haskell

# Sound Sheet 1

Read these sounds with your teacher.
Read and memorize the first group of vowel sounds and key words.
After you have memorized one group of sounds, move on to the next group.
Always start with the first group for review. Check each group as you learn it.

___ 1. ***a*** says /ă/ as in *apple*.
***a*** says /ā/ as in *baby* at the end of an open syllable *(ba/by)*.
***a*** says /ô/ as in *all* and after some *qu*'s and *w*'s as in *quality* and *water*.

___ 2. **e** says /ĕ/ as in *elephant*.
**e** says /ē/ as in *recess* at the end of an open syllable *(re/cess)*.

___ 3. ***i*** says /ĭ/ as in *it*.
***i*** says /ī/ as in *spider* at the end of an open syllable *(spi/der)*.

___ 4. ***o*** says /ŏ/ as in *ox*.
***o*** says /ō/ as in *pony* at the end of an open syllable *(po/ny)*.
***o*** says /ŭ/ as in *other*.

___ 5. ***u*** says /ŭ/ as in *up*.
***u*** says /ū/ as in *music* at the end of an open syllable *(mu/sic)*.
***u*** says /o͝o/ as in *put*.

___ 6. ***y*** says /ĭ/ as in *gym*.
***y*** says /ī/ as in *cyclone* at the end of an open syllable *(cy/clone)*.
***y*** says /ē/ as in *candy* at the end of a word.
***y*** says /ī/ as in *sky* at the end of a word.

___ 7. (***y*** is a consonant when it begins a word. **y** says /y/ as in *yes* when it begins a word.)

## Vowel-Consonant-e

___ 8. ***a***-consonant-***e*** says /ā/ as in *safe*.
***e***-consonant-***e*** says /ē/ as in *these*.
***i***-consonant-***e*** says /ī/ as in *pine*.

___ 9. ***o***-consonant-***e*** says /ō/ as in *home*.
***u***-consonant-***e*** says /ū/ as in *mule*.
***y***-consonant-***e*** says /ī/ as in *type*.

# Sound Sheet 2

Read these sounds with your teacher.
Read and memorize each sound and its key word(s).
Check each group as you learn it.

____ 1. ***sh*** says /sh/ as in *ship*.

____ 2. ***ch*** says /ch/ as in *chin*.
***ch*** says /k/ as in *chorus*.
***ch*** says /sh/ as in *Chicago*.

____ 3. ***th*** says /~~th~~/ as in *this*.
***th*** says /th/ as in *thin*.

____ 4. ***wh*** says /hw/ as in *white*.

____ 5. ***qu*** says /kw/ as in *queen*.

____ 6. ***ph*** says /f/ as in *phone*.

____ 7. ***c*** says /k/ as in *cat*.
***c*** says /s/ when it comes before e, *i*, or *y*.

____ 8. ***g*** says /g/ as in *go*.
***g*** usually says /j/ when it comes before e, *i*, or *y*. (*Get*, *give*, *girl*, and *gift* are exceptions.)

____ 9. ***s*** says /s/ as in *sat*.
***s*** between two vowels says /z/ as in *nose*.
***s*** at the end of some short words says /z/ as in *is*, *as*, and *has*.
***s*** says /z/ when it makes a word possessive, as in *Tom's cap* and *the boy's* cat.

____ 10. ***x*** says /ks/ as in *box*.
***x*** says /gz/ as in *exist*.

____ 11. ***y*** says /y/ as in *yes* when it begins a word.

____ 12. ***ed*** says /ĕd/ as in *rented*.
***ed*** says /d/ as in *sailed*.
***ed*** says /t/ as in *jumped*.

____ 13. ***ck*** says /k/ as in *black* at the end of a word or syllable directly after a single short vowel.

____ 14. ***tch*** says /ch/ as in *catch* at the end of a word or syllable directly after a single short vowel.

____ 15. ***dge*** says /j/ as in *fudge* at the end of a word or syllable directly after a single short vowel.

____ 16. ***tion*** says /shŭn/ as in *station*.
***tion*** says /chŭn/ as in *question*.

____ 17. ***sion*** says /shŭn/ as in *discussion*.
***sion*** says /zhŭn/ as in *television*.

____ 18. ***old*** says /ōld/ as in *bold*.

____ 19. ***ng*** says /ng/ as in *sing*.

# Sound Sheet 3

Read these sounds with your teacher.
Read and memorize each sound and its key word(s).
Check each group as you learn it.

The first sound given is the more common sound.

____ 1. ***ay*** says /ā/ as in *play* at the end of a word.

____ 2. ***ai*** says /ā/ as in *aid* and *sail* at the beginning or in the middle of a word.

____ 3. ***ow*** says /ō/ as in *snow*.
***ow*** says /ou/ as in *plow*.

____ 4. ***ou*** says /ou/ as in *out*.
***ou*** says /o͞o/ as in *soup*.

____ 5. ***oo*** says /o͞o/ as in *food*.
***oo*** says /o͝o/ as in *book*.

____ 6. ***oy*** says /oi/ as in *toy* at the end of a word.
***oi*** says /oi/ as in *oil* and *boil* at the beginning or in the middle of a word.

____ 7. ***oa*** says /ō/ as in *boat*.

____ 8. ***oe*** says /ō/ as in *toe*.

____ 9. ***ee*** says /ē/ as in *feed*.

____10. ***igh*** says /ī/ as in *light*.

____11. ***aw*** says /ô/ as in *saw*.

____12. ***au*** says /ô/ as in *August*.

____13. ***ie*** says /ē/ as in *chief*.
***ie*** says /ī/ as in *pie*.

____14. ***ea*** says /ē/ as in *eat*.
***ea*** says /ĕ/ as in *bread*.
***ea*** says /ā/ as in *steak*.

____15. ***eigh*** says /ā/ as in *eight*.

____16. ***ew*** says /ū/ as in *few*.
***ew*** says /o͞o/ as in *grew*.

____17. ***ey*** says /ē/ as in *valley*.
***ey*** says /ā/ as in *they*.

____18. ***ue*** says /ū/ as in *rescue*.
***ue*** says /o͞o/ as in *true*.

____19. ***ei*** says /ē/ as in *ceiling*.
***ei*** says /ā/ as in *vein*.

____20. ***eu*** says /ū/ as in *feud*.

____21. ***er*** says /er/ as in *her*.

____22. ***ir*** says /er/ as in *bird*.

____23. ***ur*** says /er/ as in *burn*.

____24. ***ear*** says /er/ as in *learn*.

____25. ***or*** says /or/ as in *hornet*.
***or*** says /er/ as in *doctor*.
***or*** after the letter *w* usually says /er/ as in *word*.

____26. ***ar*** says /är/ as in *car*.
***ar*** says /er/ as in *beggar*.

# Sounds of *c*

The consonant c has two sounds.

1. *c* before *a, o, u, l,* and *r* has the hard sound /k/.

**Copy and read these words.**

| | | |
|---|---|---|
| copy ______ | cut ______ | clap ______ |
| crust ______ | cabin ______ | coat ______ |
| cup ______ | cross ______ | |

2. *c* before *e, i,* and *y* has the soft sound /s/.

**Copy and read these words.**

| | | |
|---|---|---|
| cent ______ | city ______ | cyclone ______ |
| center ______ | circus ______ | bicycle ______ |

# Sounds of *g*

The consonant g has two sounds.

1. *g* before *a, o, u, l,* and *r* has the hard sound /g/.

**Copy and read these words.**

| | | |
|---|---|---|
| got ______ | gum ______ | glad ______ |
| grab ______ | gate ______ | good ______ |
| glide ______ | grade ______ | |

2. *g* before *e, i,* and *y* usually has the soft sound /j/.

**Copy and read these words.**

| | | |
|---|---|---|
| gem ______ | ginger ______ | gym ______ |
| gentle ______ | giant ______ | gypsy ______ |

Copy and learn the most common exceptions.

get ____________ girl ____________ give ____________

gift ____________

Read these words.
Mark the sound of *c* or *g* as hard or soft above each word. Use the following symbols.

hard *c* = /k/ hard *g* = /g/
soft *c* = /s/ soft *g* = /j/

| /k/ | /g/ | | | |
|---|---|---|---|---|
| cake | great | germ | cord | curtain |
| crisp | ginger | certain | gopher | claim |
| cloud | city | class | gamble | colder |
| general | geography | captain | goose | celery |
| glide | gelatin | cattle | coffee | got |
| catch | cinder | gorge | circus | cereal |
| giraffe | cider | gerbil | collar | giant |
| carbon | glass | ceremony | genius | glare |
| cedar | gesture | cement | calendar | ceiling |
| cellar | cymbal | grab | grace | grass |
| good | glad | certify | cycle | glory |
| celebrate | gentle | gym | century | genie |

# Sounds of *y*

*y* says /ē/ at the end of most words.

**Read, copy, and learn these words.**

| | | | | | |
|---|---|---|---|---|---|
| empty | ______ | slowly | ______ | candy | ______ |
| dirty | ______ | chilly | ______ | bushy | ______ |
| Henry | ______ | heavy | ______ | dusty | ______ |
| steamy | ______ | windy | ______ | tidy | ______ |
| copy | ______ | happy | ______ | sloppy | ______ |
| hilly | ______ | duty | ______ | carry | ______ |
| enemy | ______ | sorry | ______ | cloudy | ______ |
| rainy | ______ | sticky | ______ | rusty | ______ |
| daddy | ______ | mighty | ______ | twenty | ______ |
| sixty | ______ | fifty | ______ | ninety | ______ |

But *y* says /ī/ at the end of these one-syllable words.

| | | | | | |
|---|---|---|---|---|---|
| my | ______ | by | ______ | cry | ______ |
| why | ______ | sky | ______ | dry | ______ |
| shy | ______ | fly | ______ | spy | ______ |
| try | ______ | fry | ______ | spry | ______ |
| pry | ______ | sly | ______ | ply | ______ |

## Sounds of *ow*

If *ow* in the words below sounds like /ō/ as in *snow,* write an X on the line.
If *ow* in the words below sounds like /ou/ as in *plow,* write a ✓ on the line.

| | | | |
|---|---|---|---|
| _X_ show | _✓_ how | ____ grow | ____ own |
| ____ clown | ____ crow | ____ brown | ____ howl |
| ____ crowd | ____ low | ____ thrown | ____ town |
| ____ power | ____ blown | ____ cow | ____ drown |
| ____ shown | ____ arrow | ____ glow | ____ follow |
| ____ gown | ____ grown | ____ flow | ____ crown |
| ____ window | ____ tower | ____ vowel | ____ shower |
| ____ fellow | ____ flower | ____ towel | ____ throw |
| ____ shadow | ____ narrow | ____ scowl | ____ tomorrow |

## Sounds of *oo*

If *oo* in the words below sounds like /o͞o/ as in *food,* write an X on the line.
If *oo* in the words below sounds like /o͝o/ as in *book,* write a ✓ on the line.

| | | | |
|---|---|---|---|
| _X_ moon | _✓_ look | ____ broom | ____ good |
| ____ droop | ____ hood | ____ smooth | ____ stood |
| ____ wood | ____ stoop | ____ proof | ____ cook |
| ____ hook | ____ shook | ____ pool | ____ fool |
| ____ book | ____ boot | ____ spool | ____ spook |
| ____ spoon | ____ swoon | ____ noodle | ____ noose |
| ____ doom | ____ brook | ____ cool | ____ room |
| ____ crook | ____ loose | ____ nook | ____ boost |
| ____ wool | ____ shoot | ____ foot | ____ soot |

# Sounds of *ea*

If *ea* in the words below sounds like /ē/ as in *eat*, write an X on the line.
If *ea* in the words below sounds like /ĕ/ as in *bread*, write a ✓ on the line.

| | | | |
|---|---|---|---|
| _X_ beach | _✓_ head | ____ meat | ____ weak |
| ____ ready | ____ sea | ____ sweater | ____ peace |
| ____ leaf | ____ dread | ____ spread | ____ dear |
| ____ health | ____ cream | ____ thread | ____ sweat |
| ____ neat | ____ lease | ____ pleasure | ____ dream |
| ____ heavy | ____ deaf | ____ rear | ____ feature |
| ____ sneak | ____ plead | ____ wealth | ____ tease |
| ____ heat | ____ meant | ____ feather | ____ repeat |
| ____ leather | ____ peanut | ____ feast | ____ weather |
| ____ instead | ____ breath | ____ team | ____ measure |
| ____ steady | ____ crease | ____ bread | ____ treasure |
| ____ fear | ____ deal | ____ hear | ____ death |

*ea* sounds like /ā/ in these words.

Copy and read the words.

| | | |
|---|---|---|
| bear ________ | pear ________ | wear ________ |
| tear ________ | swear________ | steak ________ |
| great ________ | break________ | |

Use a separate sheet of paper. Use each word in an original sentence.

# Other Sounds for the Vowels *a* and *o*

**Read, copy, and learn the words.**

1. *a* usually says /ô/ when followed by *l*.

| | | |
|---|---|---|
| ball ________ | halt ________ | walnut ________ |
| call ________ | walk ________ | waltz ________ |
| fall ________ | talk ________ | wallet ________ |
| hall ________ | chalk ________ | wallop ________ |
| wall ________ | stalk ________ | walrus ________ |
| tall ________ | | |
| small ________ | | |

2. *a* usually says /ä/ after *w*.

| | | |
|---|---|---|
| wad ________ | wan ________ | wand ________ |
| wander ________ | waddle ________ | waffle ________ |
| watch ________ | watt ________ | wasp ________ |

3. *a* usually says /ô/ when followed by *r*.

| | | |
|---|---|---|
| war ________ | warble ________ | ward ________ |
| warden ________ | warm ________ | warp ________ |
| wart ________ | wardrobe ________ | award ________ |
| reward ________ | swarm ________ | |

# Other Sounds for the Vowels *a* and *o* (continued)

4. *a* usually says /ä/ after *qu*.

squat ____________ squall ____________ squad ____________
squash ____________

*a* after *qu* says /ô/ if it is *r*-controlled.

quart ____________ quarter ____________ quarrel ____________

5. *a* says /ŭ/ when it is at the beginning of these words.

ahead ____________ aboard ____________ abound ____________
about ____________ above ____________ across ____________
afar ____________ again ____________ alike ____________
alive ____________ along ____________ among ____________
around ____________ award ____________ away ____________
awhile ____________ asleep ____________ afloat ____________
adrift ____________ ashore ____________ aware ____________
amend ____________ amaze ____________ afraid ____________

6. The underlined *a*'s in the following words say /ŭ/.

banana ____________ China ____________ coma ____________
comma ____________ idea ____________ India ____________
panda ____________ parade ____________ soda ____________
sofa ____________ umbrella ____________ vanilla ____________

7. *o* says /ŭ/ in these words.

| | | | | | |
|---|---|---|---|---|---|
| other | ______ | oven | ______ | won | ______ |
| mother | ______ | dozen | ______ | wonder | ______ |
| brother | ______ | love | ______ | onion | ______ |
| another | ______ | dove | ______ | Monday | ______ |
| smother | ______ | glove | ______ | month | ______ |
| come | ______ | shove | ______ | nothing | ______ |
| some | ______ | front | ______ | tongue | ______ |
| done | ______ | ton | ______ | | |
| none | ______ | son | ______ | | |

*o* says /ŭ/ in these unaccented syllables.

| | | | | | |
|---|---|---|---|---|---|
| lemon | ______ | somebody | ______ | lion | ______ |
| diamond | ______ | parrot | ______ | wagon | ______ |

8. *o* is not heard in the second syllable of these words.

| | | | | | |
|---|---|---|---|---|---|
| lesson | ______ | atom | ______ | bottom | ______ |
| button | ______ | carton | ______ | cotton | ______ |
| mutton | ______ | glutton | ______ | ribbon | ______ |

# Review of Sounds

List all the ways these sounds can be spelled.

/ā/: ________, ________, ________, ________, ________, ________, ________, ________.

/ē/: ________, ________, ________, ________, ________, ________, ________, ________.

/ī/: ________, ________, ________, ________, ________, ________.

/ō/: ________, ________, ________, ________, ________.

/ū/: ________, ________, ________, ________, ________.

/o͞o/: ________, ________, ________, ________.

/o͝o/: ________, ________.

/ô/: ________, ________, ________.

/ou/: ________, ________.

/oi/: ________, ________.

/er/: ________, ________, ________, ________, ________, ________.

/ĭ/: ________, ________.

# Syllables

Read, copy, and learn.

A syllable is part of a word with a vowel in it.

______________________________________

There are six kinds of syllables.

______________________________________

| | |
|---|---|
| I. **Closed syllable** | I. ____________________ |
| A. It ends with a consonant. | A. ____________________ |
| | ____________________ |
| B. The vowel has a short sound. | B. ____________________ |
| | ____________________ |

Copy the examples.

| | | |
|---|---|---|
| 1. sŭd | 3. hăb | 5. trŭm |
| 2. dĕn | 4. ĭt | 6. pĕt |
| 1. __________ | 3. __________ | 5. __________ |
| 2. __________ | 4. __________ | 6. __________ |

Make words from these closed syllables. Then read the words.

| | | | | | | | | | |
|---|---|---|---|---|---|---|---|---|---|
| cab | + | in | = | cabin | him | + | self | = | himself |
| sub | + | mit | = | submit | in | + | vent | = | inwent |
| con | + | test | = | contest | vis | + | it | = | visit |
| trum | + | pet | = | trumpet | ad | + | mit | = | admit |
| nap | + | kin | = | napkin | con | + | test | = | contest |
| sud | + | den | = | sudden | sun | + | set | = | sunset |
| mag | + | net | = | magnet | prob | + | lem | = | problem |

Read, copy, and learn.

II. **Open syllable**

A. It ends with a vowel.

B. The vowel has a long sound. (The long sound of a vowel is usually the name of the vowel.)

II. ____________________

A. ____________________

B. ____________________

____________________

Copy the examples.

| | | |
|---|---|---|
| 1. hī | 3. zē | 5. bā |
| 2. fī | 4. rō | 6. bȳ |
| 1. ________ | 3. ________ | 5. ________ |
| 2. ________ | 4. ________ | 6. ________ |

Make words from these open syllables. Then read the words.

| | | | | |
|---|---|---|---|---|
| cra | + | zy | = | crazy |
| ho | + | bo | = | hobo |
| i | + | cy | = | icy |
| la | + | dy | = | lady |
| i | + | vy | = | ivy |
| po | + | lo | = | polo |
| ti | + | dy | = | tidy |
| sto | + | ny | = | Stony |
| pho | + | to | = | ________ |
| re | + | ply | = | ________ |

Read, copy, and learn.

III. **Vowel-consonant-e syllable** III. ______________

A. The final e is silent. A. ______________

B. The silent e at the end of the word makes the vowel before it have a long sound. B. ______________

______________

______________

______________

Copy the examples.

1. tīme̸ 3. cūbe̸ 5. thēse̸

2. nōte̸ 4. strīpe̸ 6. shāme̸

1. ______________ 3. ______________ 5. ______________

2. ______________ 4. ______________ 6. ______________

Make these closed-syllable words into vowel-consonant-*e* words by adding a silent *e*. Then read each pair of words orally.

| | | | | | |
|---|---|---|---|---|---|
| can | cane | rat | ______ | rod | ______ |
| bit | ______ | van | ______ | dim | ______ |
| cub | ______ | win | ______ | hop | ______ |
| pan | ______ | cut | ______ | us | ______ |
| plan | ______ | rip | ______ | slim | ______ |
| not | ______ | cap | ______ | slop | ______ |
| rob | ______ | grim | ______ | twin | ______ |
| pin | ______ | slat | ______ | strip | ______ |

*Name the Syllables*

1. **Underline all the sounded vowels. Cross out silent *e*'s. Do not count *u* as a vowel when it appears after *q*.**
2. **Label all the syllables:** o = open
   c = closed
   vce = vowel-consonant-e
3. **Read the syllables orally.**

| | | | | | | | |
|---|---|---|---|---|---|---|---|
| tob | c | pro | ______ | mave | ______ | chate | ______ |
| thive | vce | se | ______ | thuse | ______ | bri | ______ |
| cra | o | cu | ______ | smu | ______ | clabe | ______ |
| in | ______ | ob | ______ | whe | ______ | stume | ______ |
| chib | ______ | sepe | ______ | shune | ______ | quete | ______ |
| cun | ______ | dev | ______ | sym | ______ | hib | ______ |
| blake | ______ | gla | ______ | ume | ______ | quave | ______ |
| flobe | ______ | fe | ______ | shuve | ______ | bru | ______ |
| re | ______ | chob | ______ | sleme | ______ | pos | ______ |
| fro | ______ | glov | ______ | tove | ______ | ste | ______ |
| brune | ______ | glan | ______ | blist | ______ | ti | ______ |
| flin | ______ | deve | ______ | be | ______ | ret | ______ |
| grun | ______ | dro | ______ | shive | ______ | heb | ______ |
| hove | ______ | ste | ______ | swem | ______ | de | ______ |

Read, copy, and learn.

IV. **Diphthong syllable**

A. It has a special sound.

B. It usually has two vowels together. (You have learned the sounds on Sound Sheet 3.)

IV. ______________________

A. ______________________

B. ______________________

______________________

Copy the examples.

| | | |
|---|---|---|
| 1. rain | 3. greet | 5. bread |
| 2. play | 4. snow | 6. light |
| 1. __________ | 3. __________ | 5. __________ |
| 2. __________ | 4. __________ | 6. __________ |

*Name the Syllables*

1. Underline all the sounded vowels and diphthongs. Cross out silent *e*'s.
2. Label all the syllables: o = open; c = closed; vce = vowel-consonant-e; d = diphthong
3. Read the syllables orally.

| | | | | | | | |
|---|---|---|---|---|---|---|---|
| pen | c | com | ______ | zai | ______ | su | ______ |
| roo | d | be | ______ | choi | ______ | wib | ______ |
| whi | ______ | bline | ______ | hope | ______ | bow | ______ |
| dro | ______ | teigh | ______ | tay | ______ | re | ______ |
| ad | ______ | mup | ______ | zeet | ______ | jine | ______ |

Read, copy, and learn.

V. **r-combination syllable** V. ______________________

A. This syllable always has at least one vowel followed by r. A. ______________________

______________________

______________________

B. The vowel-r combinations are ar, er, ir, or, ur, and ear. (You should already know the sounds these vowel-r combinations make.) B. ______________________

______________________

______________________

______________________

Copy the examples.

1. car
2. sĭs/ter
3. bird
4. horn
5. burn
6. earth

1. ______________ 3. ______________ 5. ______________

2. ______________ 4. ______________ 6. ______________

Read these vowel-*r* combinations in words.

| | | | | | |
|---|---|---|---|---|---|
| ar: | star | ir: | girl | ur: | turn |
| er: | person | or: | corn | ear: | learn |

Write your own words that have a vowel-*r* combination.

| | | | |
|---|---|---|---|
| ar: | ______________ | ar: | ______________ |
| er: | ______________ | er: | ______________ |
| ir: | ______________ | ir: | ______________ |
| or: | ______________ | or: | ______________ |
| ur: | ______________ | ur: | ______________ |
| ear: | ______________ | ear: | ______________ |

Read, copy, and learn.

VI. <u>**Consonant-le syllable**</u>

A. This syllable always comes at the end of a word.

B. The final <u>e</u> in this syllable is silent.

C. The syllables are <u>ble</u>, <u>dle</u>, <u>fle</u>, <u>gle</u>, <u>kle</u>, <u>ple</u>, <u>tle</u>, <u>zle</u>, and <u>stle</u>.

VI. ______________________

A. ______________________

______________________

______________________

B. ______________________

______________________

C. ______________________

______________________

______________________

Copy the examples.

| | | |
|---|---|---|
| 1. bub/ble | 3. strug/gle | 5. set/tle |
| 2. cra/dle | 4. star/tle | 6. sta/ble |
| 1. ____________ | 3. ____________ | 5. ____________ |
| 2. ____________ | 4. ____________ | 6. ____________ |

1. In the following words, start with the last letter. Count back three letters and draw a line (/). You have found the consonant-*le* syllable at the end of the word.
2. Mark the first vowel in each word long (¯) or short (˘).
3. Read the words.

Remember: The first syllable is closed if it ends with a consonant. The vowel has a short sound.

The first syllable is open if it ends with a vowel. The vowel has a long sound (it says its own name).

| | | | |
|---|---|---|---|
| băttle | staple | kettle | sniffle |
| rifle | puzzle | candle | riddle |
| kindle | idle | tremble | tumble |
| thimble | simple | fizzle | dimple |
| bundle | jungle | table | topple |

*Name the Syllables*

1. Underline all the sounded vowels and diphthongs. Cross out silent *e*'s.
2. Label all the syllables:

| | |
|---|---|
| o = open | d = diphthong |
| c = closed | r = r-combination |
| vce = vowel-consonant-e | c-le = consonant-le |

3. Read the syllables orally.

| | | | | | | | |
|---|---|---|---|---|---|---|---|
| chaim | d | blet | ______ | pron | ______ | droan | ______ |
| gle | c-le | droak | ______ | cur | ______ | whime | ______ |
| orch | r | baun | ______ | kle | ______ | spe | ______ |
| ran | ______ | heve | ______ | lail | ______ | ver | ______ |
| mir | ______ | ple | ______ | ke | ______ | reem | ______ |
| shois | ______ | frar | ______ | pligh | ______ | squir | ______ |
| chode | ______ | sten | ______ | cha | ______ | dle | ______ |
| tle | ______ | bew | ______ | lipe | ______ | cod | ______ |
| thi | ______ | di | ______ | toap | ______ | ney | ______ |
| zait | ______ | irst | ______ | pher | ______ | dow | ______ |
| shan | ______ | dir | ______ | glos | ______ | roy | ______ |
| sha | ______ | fra | ______ | grale | ______ | cho | ______ |
| shaun | ______ | hoap | ______ | frane | ______ | nay | ______ |
| gru | ______ | tun | ______ | chi | ______ | yane | ______ |
| zle | ______ | yin | ______ | chim | ______ | por | ______ |
| whee | ______ | neal | ______ | nil | ______ | su | ______ |
| ird | ______ | brafe | ______ | smar | ______ | ait | ______ |
| stle | ______ | boo | ______ | sile | ______ | si | ______ |
| main | ______ | bool | ______ | pir | ______ | sine | ______ |
| mait | ______ | erst | ______ | gral | ______ | stur | ______ |

# Syllabication
## (Dividing Words into Syllables)

1. To divide a word into syllables, first underline all the sounded vowels and dipthongs. If the word ends with a single e, cross out the e because e at the end of the word is silent.

   Copy.

   1. sudden    2. magnet    3. pancake

   1. ______    2. ______    3. ______

2. Label all the vowels and consonants, starting with the first vowel in the word.

   Copy.

   1. sudden    2. magnet    3. pancake
      vccvc        vccvc        vccvc

   1. ______    2. ______    3. ______
      ______       ______       ______

3. Do you find a pattern that looks like this: VCCV? Put a box around it.

   Copy.

   1. sudden    2. magnet    3. pancake
      vccvc        vccvc        vccvc

   1. ______    2. ______    3. ______
      ______       ______       ______

4. Divide between the two consonants: VC/CV.

   Copy.

   1. sud/den    2. mag/net    3. pan/cake
      vc/cv         vc/cv         vc/cv

   1. ______    2. ______    3. ______
      ______       ______       ______

# Syllabication (continued)

Read, copy, and learn.

Remember:

1. **When two consonants come between two vowels,** divide between the two consonants.

1. ______________________________

______________________________

Divide the words below.

1. Underline all the sounded vowels.
2. Label all the vowels and consonants starting with the first vowel in the word.
3. Find the pattern, VCCV, and put a box around it.
4. Divide between the consonants.
5. Label the syllables: o, c, or r.

| | | | |
|---|---|---|---|
| c r<br>din\|ner<br>VC\|CV C | blotter | rabbit | hammer |
| shabby | invent | supper | planning |
| sudden | flatten | muffin | dentist |
| picnic | napkin | silver | harvest |
| number | velvet | sister | contest |

Read, copy, and learn.

II. A. **<u>When only one consonant comes between two vowels,</u>** VCV, divide after the first vowel: V/CV.

B. If you hear a word that you do not know, divide after the consonant: VC/V.

II. A. ________________________________________

________________________________________

B. ________________________________________

________________________________________

Remember: In syllables that end with a vowel, the vowel usually has a long sound. These are open syllables.

In syllables that end with a consonant, the vowel usually has a short sound. These are closed syllables.

Divide the words below.

1. Underline all the vowels.
2. Label all the vowels and consonants starting with the first vowel in the word.
3. Find the pattern, VCV, and put a box around it.
4. Divide after the first vowel: V/CV. If you do not hear a word that you know, divide after the consonant: VC/V.
5. Label the syllables: o, c, or r.

| | | | |
|---|---|---|---|
| o c<br>si/lent<br>VCVCC | atom | navy | unit |
| travel | seven | final | lilac |
| timid | robin | razor | level |
| salad | music | hotel | planet |

# Syllabication (continued)

Read, copy, and learn.

III. A. **<u>When three consonants come between two vowels,</u>** VCCCV, divide after the first consonant: VC/CCV.

B. If you hear a word that you do not know, divide after the second consonant: VCC/CV.

C. Do not divide between consonant blends such as <u>sh</u>, <u>ph</u>, <u>ch</u>, <u>st</u>, <u>br</u>, <u>sp</u>, and <u>gl</u>.

III. A. ____________________________________________

____________________________________________

B. ____________________________________________

____________________________________________

C. ____________________________________________

____________________________________________

Divide the words below.

1. Underline all the sounded vowels and diphthongs. Cross out silent *e*'s.
2. Label all the vowels and consonants starting with the first vowel in the word.
3. Find the pattern, VCCCV, and put a box around it.
4. Divide after the first consonant: VC/CCV. If you do not hear a word that you know, divide after the second consonant: VCC/CV.
5. Remember that consonant blends such as *sh, st,* and *br* are not divided.
6. Label the syllables: o, c, vc<u>e</u>, d, r, or c-<u>le</u>.

| | | | |
|---|---|---|---|
| c c-le<br>sam/ple (VC/CCV) | subtract | partner | mischief |
| hungry | simply | pilgrim | contract |
| extreme | complete | pumpkin | orphan |
| athlete | monster | transfer | apprehend |

# Suffixes

Read, copy, and learn.

A suffix is an ending added to a word. It changes the meaning of the word. A word without a suffix is called a base word.

______________________________

______________________________

______________________________

Some suffixes begin with vowels.

Read, copy, and learn.

| | | | | | | | |
|---|---|---|---|---|---|---|---|
| ing | ________ | er | ________ | able | ________ | est | ________ |
| ed | ________ | al | ________ | ible | ________ | ist | ________ |
| y | ________ | en | ________ | ish | ________ | | |

Some suffixes begin with consonants.

Read, copy, and learn.

| | | | | | | | |
|---|---|---|---|---|---|---|---|
| ly | ________ | ment | ________ | ness | ________ | less | ________ |
| ful | ________ | | | | | | |

## The Suffix *-ed*

The suffix *-ed* makes a verb express the past tense. Past tense shows that something has already happened. The suffix *-ed* has three sounds.

*ed* says /ĕd/ as in *rented.*
*ed* says /d/ as in *sailed.*
*ed* says /t/ as in *jumped* .

Read the words in the left column. What sound does *ed* have in each word? After you have decided what sound *ed* has in each word, place that word in the correct column. Underline the base word once and the suffix twice.

| | /ĕd/ | /d/ | /t/ |
|---|---|---|---|
| frosted | frosted | stayed | |
| stayed | | | |
| growled | | | |
| opened | | | |
| showed | | | |
| waited | | | |
| washed | | | |
| handed | | | |
| talked | | | |
| twisted | | | |
| mended | | | |
| blinked | | | |
| grunted | | | |
| added | | | |
| masked | | | |
| needed | | | |

# Sight Word List 1

Read these words. Copy any word you cannot spell.

| | | | |
|---|---|---|---|
| a | __________ | does | __________ |
| the | __________ | said | __________ |
| to | __________ | there | __________ |
| do | __________ | where | __________ |
| no | __________ | were | __________ |
| go | __________ | what | __________ |
| so | __________ | want | __________ |
| he | __________ | have | __________ |
| me | __________ | some | __________ |
| she | __________ | come | __________ |
| we | __________ | are | __________ |
| be | __________ | you | __________ |
| of | __________ | your | __________ |
| was | __________ | says | __________ |
| too | __________ | goes | __________ |

**After you know how to spell all the words on Sight Word List 1, use a separate sheet of paper to write the sentences dictated by your teacher.**[1]

[1] Dictate sentences from the list on page 33 in *How to Teach Spelling.*

# *ff, ll, ss* Spelling Rule

**Read and learn the rule.**

One-syllable words that end in *f, l,* or *s* double the final *f, l,* or *s.*

**Read, copy, and learn these words.**

| | | |
|---|---|---|
| off ________ | ball ________ | dress ________ |
| huff ________ | hall ________ | press ________ |
| puff ________ | bell ________ | class ________ |
| cuff ________ | dull ________ | cross ________ |
| cliff ________ | fill ________ | fuss ________ |
| stuff ________ | spell ________ | toss ________ |
| gruff ________ | yell ________ | boss ________ |
| stiff ________ | smell ________ | brass ________ |
| bluff ________ | wall ________ | chess ________ |
| sniff ________ | thrill ________ | stress ________ |

**Read, copy, and learn the exceptions to this rule.**

| | | | |
|---|---|---|---|
| if ________ | as ________ | is ________ | us ________ |
| of ________ | has ________ | his ________ | bus ________ |
| elf ________ | was ________ | this ________ | plus ________ |
| chef ________ | gas ________ | | |
| pal ________ | yes ________ | | |

**Use a separate sheet of paper to write the words, phrases, and sentences dictated by your teacher. This dictation will check your ability to spell words that end in *ff, ll,* and *ss.*[1]**

[1] Dictate words, phrases, and sentences from the lists on pages 34 and 35 in *How to Teach Spelling.*

# *ld, nd, st* Spelling Rule

**Read and learn the rule.**

The vowels *i* and *o* in one-syllable words that end in *ld, nd,* and *st* may have a long sound.

**Read, copy, and learn these words.**

| *ld* | | *nd* | | *st* | |
|---|---|---|---|---|---|
| old | ____________ | bind | ____________ | host | ____________ |
| bold | ____________ | blind | ____________ | most | ____________ |
| cold | ____________ | behind | ____________ | post | ____________ |
| hold | ____________ | find | ____________ | ghost | ____________ |
| gold | ____________ | grind | ____________ | | |
| mold | ____________ | kind | ____________ | | |
| fold | ____________ | mind | ____________ | | |
| sold | ____________ | wind | ____________ | | |
| told | ____________ | | | | |
| scold | ____________ | | | | |
| child | ____________ | | | | |
| mild | ____________ | | | | |
| wild | ____________ | | | | |

**Use a separate sheet of paper to write the words, phrases, and sentences dictated by your teacher. This dictation will check your ability to spell words that end in *ld, nd,* and *st.*[1]**

[1] Dictate words, phrases, and sentences from the lists on page 36 in *How to Teach Spelling*.

# Sight Word List 2

Read and copy these words. Can you spell every word? ________

| | | | | | |
|---|---|---|---|---|---|
| one | ________ | live | ________ | they | ________ |
| once | ________ | could | ________ | shall | ________ |
| only | ________ | would | ________ | sew | ________ |
| two | ________ | should | ________ | eye | ________ |
| shoe | ________ | again | ________ | egg | ________ |
| who | ________ | against | ________ | door | ________ |
| whose | ________ | put | ________ | floor | ________ |
| whom | ________ | push | ________ | four | ________ |
| any | ________ | pull | ________ | pour | ________ |
| many | ________ | full | ________ | pint | ________ |
| gone | ________ | wear | ________ | both | ________ |
| none | ________ | tear | ________ | father | ________ |
| done | ________ | swear | ________ | parent | ________ |
| give | ________ | bear | ________ | been | ________ |

**After you know how to spell all the words on Sight Word List 2, use a separate sheet of paper to write the sentences dictated by your teacher.**[1]

[1] Dictate sentences from the list on page 38 in *How to Teach Spelling*.

# /k/—Spelled *k* and *ck*

The following generalizations will help you learn which letter(s) to use at the end of a word or syllable for the /k/ sound.

**Read, copy, and learn.**

1. /k/ can be spelled k or ck.
2. Use ck at the end of a word or syllable directly after a single short vowel.
3. Use k after a consonant, after a long-vowel sound, and after two vowels.

1. ______________________________

2. ______________________________

______________________________

3. ______________________________

______________________________

**Write the words in the correct column.**

| | | | |
|---|---|---|---|
| check | clock | crack | duck |
| speak | peek | smoke | speck |
| look | back | pink | sink |

| *k* | *ck* |
|---|---|
| speak | check |
| | |
| | |
| | |
| | |
| | |

**Use a separate sheet of paper.**

1. Write the *k—ck* generalizations from memory.
2. Give at least five examples of words spelled with *k* and *ck*.

# /k/—Spelled *k* and *ck* (continued)

Fill in the blanks with either *k* or *ck*. Be sure you make words that sound familiar. Then read the words.

| ta_ck_ | li___ | tan___ | tra___ | du___ |
|---|---|---|---|---|
| drin___ | qua___ | ro___ | blin___ | pri___ |
| bro___e | smo___ | spea___ | par___ | ra___e |
| so___ | tru___ | pi___ | lea___ | lu___ |
| mil___ | ne___ | stor___ | lo___et | che___ |
| clo___ | hul___ | mar___ | sta___ | stri___e |
| ban___ | fli___ | bu___et | stin___ | sti___ |
| spoo___ | bi___e | min___ | dar___ | thi___ |
| ba___e | ba___ | pin___ | bla___ | blan___ |
| si___ | sho___ | bul___ | ro___er | spar___ |

**Use a separate sheet of paper to write the words, phrases, and sentences dictated by your teacher. This dictation will check your ability to spell words that end in *k* and *ck*.**[1]

[1] Dictate words, phrases, and sentences from the lists on pages 39, 40, and 41 in *How to Teach Spelling*.

# /ĭk/—Spelled *ic*

You already know that the /k/ sound directly after a single short vowel is spelled *ck*. Words with two or more syllables usually use *c* for the final /k/ sound.

**Read, copy, and learn these words.**

| | | |
|---|---|---|
| attic__________ | athletic__________ | gymnastic__________ |
| magic__________ | plastic__________ | patriotic__________ |
| music__________ | electric__________ | antibiotic__________ |
| picnic__________ | elastic__________ | epidemic__________ |
| fabric__________ | gigantic__________ | arithmetic__________ |
| metric__________ | frantic__________ | domestic__________ |
| public__________ | traffic__________ | automatic__________ |
| Arctic__________ | magnetic__________ | rhythmic__________ |
| critic__________ | olympic__________ | democratic__________ |
| garlic__________ | ceramic__________ | mechanic__________ |
| panic__________ | Atlantic__________ | mathematic__________ |
| topic__________ | Pacific__________ | romantic__________ |
| comic__________ | heroic__________ | scientific__________ |
| cubic__________ | historic__________ | sympathetic__________ |
| basic__________ | allergic__________ | systematic__________ |
| atomic__________ | clinic__________ | terrific__________ |
| tragic__________ | scenic__________ | specific__________ |

**Read and learn.**

When adding a suffix that begins with *e, i,* or *y,* you must insert a *k* before the suffix to prevent the final *c* from being pronounced /s/.

| | |
|---|---|
| picnic—picnicked—picnicking | panic—panicked—panicking |
| mimic—mimicked—mimicking | traffic—trafficked—trafficking |

# /ch/—Spelled *ch* and *tch*

The following generalizations will help you learn which letters to use at the end of a word or syllable for the /ch/ sound.

**Read, copy, and learn.**

1. /ch/ can be spelled ch or tch.
2. Use tch at the end of a word or syllable directly after a single short vowel.
3. Use ch at the beginning of a word, after a consonant, and after two vowels.

1. ______________________________

2. ______________________________

______________________________

3. ______________________________

______________________________

**Write the words in the correct column.**

| | | | | |
|---|---|---|---|---|
| lunch | match | perch | itch | porch |
| stitch | pinch | ditch | scratch | teach |

| *ch* | *tch* |
|---|---|
| __________ | __________ |
| __________ | __________ |
| __________ | __________ |
| __________ | __________ |
| __________ | __________ |

**Read, copy, and learn the exceptions.**

| | | | | | |
|---|---|---|---|---|---|
| much | __________ | which | __________ | attach | __________ |
| such | __________ | sandwich | __________ | detach | __________ |
| rich | __________ | ostrich | __________ | | |

Use a separate sheet of paper.

1. Write the *ch—tch* generalizations from memory.
2. Give at least five examples of words spelled with *ch* and *tch*.

Fill in the blanks with either *ch* or *tch*. Be sure you make words that sound familiar. Then read the words.

| | | | | |
|---|---|---|---|---|
| hun____ | ma____ | pi____ | ben____ | ca____ |
| wi____ | dren____ | clu____ | pea____ | di____ |
| sna____ | crun____ | sten____ | bun____ | ha____ |
| i____ | tren____ | cou____ | hi____ | prea____ |
| coa____ | la____ | bea____ | swi____ | pa____ |
| grou____ | fe____ | mar____ | sti____ | pin____ |
| ba____ | mun____ | ran____ | Du____ | per____ |
| por____ | scor____ | scra____ | scree____ | pou____ |

**Use a separate sheet of paper to write the words, phrases, and sentences dictated by your teacher. This dictation will check your ability to spell words that end in *ch* and *tch*.**[1]

[1] Dictate words, phrases, and sentences from the lists on pages 43 and 44 in *How to Teach Spelling*.

# /j/—Spelled *ge* and *dge*

The following generalizations will help you learn which letters to use at the end of a word or syllable for the /j/ sound.

Read, copy, and learn.

1. /j/ can be spelled ge or dge.
2. Use dge at the end of a word or syllable directly after a single short vowel.
3. Use ge after a consonant, after a long-vowel sound, and after two vowels.

1. ______________________________

2. ______________________________

______________________________

3. ______________________________

______________________________

Write the words in the correct column.

| | | | | | |
|---|---|---|---|---|---|
| bridge | wedge | fudge | fringe | change | cage |
| page | range | badge | age | huge | hedge |
| smudge | dodge | stage | judge | | |

| *ge* | *dge* |
|---|---|
| ____________ | ____________ |
| ____________ | ____________ |
| ____________ | ____________ |
| ____________ | ____________ |
| ____________ | ____________ |
| ____________ | ____________ |
| ____________ | ____________ |
| ____________ | ____________ |

Read, copy, and learn these words.

partridge ____________________ knowledge ____________________

cartridge ____________________ acknowledge ____________________

porridge ____________________

Use a separate sheet of paper.

1. Write the *ge—dge* generalizations from memory.
2. Give at least five examples of words spelled with *ge* and *dge*.
3. Write five original sentences using *ge* and *dge* words. Use as many of the following words as you can: partridge, cartridge, porridge, knowledge, and acknowledge.

Fill in the blanks with either *ge* or *dge*. Be sure you make words that sound familiar. Then read the words.

| | | | | |
|---|---|---|---|---|
| ra_____ | ba_____ | frin_____ | he_____ | hin_____ |
| a_____ | ca_____ | hu_____ | le_____ | sta_____ |
| dre_____ | we_____ | bar_____ | gru_____ | smu_____ |
| ver_____ | ple_____ | lar_____ | ur_____ | ran_____ |
| gou_____ | gor_____ | nu_____ | chan_____ | lo_____ |
| ju_____ | do_____ | tru_____ | ri_____ | fu_____ |
| spon_____ | mer_____ | ga_____ | arran_____ | stran_____ |
| knowle_____ | cartri_____ | porri_____ | partri_____ | for_____ |

**Use a separate sheet of paper to write the words, phrases, and sentences dictated by your teacher. This dictation will check your ability to spell words that end in *ge* and *dge*.**[1]

[1] Dictate words, phrases, and sentences from the lists on pages 44, 45, and 46 in *How to Teach Spelling*.

## /ĭj/—Spelled *age*

The /ĭj/ sound at the end of a word is spelled *age*.

**Read, copy, and learn these words.**

| | | | |
|---|---|---|---|
| baggage | ________________ | discourage | ________________ |
| cabbage | ________________ | hostage | ________________ |
| cottage | ________________ | heritage | ________________ |
| luggage | ________________ | image | ________________ |
| encourage | ________________ | language | ________________ |
| courage | ________________ | message | ________________ |
| garbage | ________________ | package | ________________ |
| beverage | ________________ | passage | ________________ |
| damage | ________________ | voyage | ________________ |
| manage | ________________ | postage | ________________ |
| mileage | ________________ | salvage | ________________ |
| acreage | ________________ | sausage | ________________ |
| footage | ________________ | savage | ________________ |
| yardage | ________________ | shortage | ________________ |
| average | ________________ | voltage | ________________ |
| advantage | ________________ | storage | ________________ |
| bandage | ________________ | village | ________________ |

Copy and learn these two exceptions:

college ________________ privilege ________________

**Use a separate sheet of paper to write the phrases and sentences dictated by your teacher. This dictation will check your ability to spell words that end in *age*.**[1]

[1] Dictate phrases and sentences from the lists on pages 47 and 48 in *How to Teach Spelling*.

## Sight Word List 3

Read and copy these words. Learn to spell them.

| | | |
|---|---|---|
| add ____________ | beauty ____________ | easy ____________ |
| odd ____________ | animal ____________ | woman ____________ |
| answer ____________ | minute ____________ | women ____________ |
| carry ____________ | people ____________ | above ____________ |
| marry ____________ | police ____________ | canoe ____________ |
| hurry ____________ | hero ____________ | ocean ____________ |
| merry ____________ | during ____________ | change ____________ |
| ferry ____________ | laugh ____________ | strange ____________ |
| berry ____________ | walk ____________ | piano ____________ |
| buy ____________ | talk ____________ | promise ____________ |
| busy ____________ | chalk ____________ | board ____________ |
| bury ____________ | lose ____________ | mitt ____________ |
| dye ____________ | loose ____________ | almost ____________ |
| die ____________ | very ____________ | always ____________ |
| color ____________ | every ____________ | already ____________ |
| pretty ____________ | else ____________ | all right ____________ |

**After you know how to spell all the words on Sight Word List 3, use a separate sheet of paper to write the sentences dictated by your teacher.**[1]

[1] Dictate sentences from the list on pages 49 and 50 in *How to Teach Spelling*.

# /ou/—Spelled *ou* and *ow*

Read, copy, and learn.

1. Use ou at the beginning or in the middle of a word unless the /ou/ sound is followed by a single n, l, er, or el; then use ow.

| | | |
|---|---|---|
| shout | fowl | flower |
| flour | growl | power |
| ground | scowl | tower |
| down | | towel |
| clown | | vowel |
| brown | | trowel |

2. Use ow at the end of a word for the /ou/ sound.

| | | |
|---|---|---|
| cow | now | brow |
| how | plow | allow |

Read, copy, and learn the exceptions.

| | |
|---|---|
| powder | chowder |
| coward | foul |
| crowd | |

Fill in the blanks with either *ou* or *ow*. Then read the words. Place a check in front of the words that are exceptions to the generalizations.

| | | | |
|---|---|---|---|
| sc____t | br____n | cl____n | l____d |
| s____r | gr____l | st____t | h____ |
| tr____sers | spr____t | ar____nd | m____se |
| f____nd | m____th | ch____der | sl____ch |
| dr____n | c____nt | fl____er | fl____r |
| c____ard | b____nce | h____se | cr____n |
| p____er | t____el | pl____ | bl____se |
| s____nd | sh____er | cr____d | p____nce |
| t____er | ____r | all____ | gr____nd |
| tr____el | p____der | cr____ch | fr____n |

**Use a separate sheet of paper to write the words, phrases, and sentences dictated by your teacher. This dictation will check your ability to spell words with *ou* and *ow*.**[1]

[1] Dictate words, phrases, and sentences from the lists on pages 51 and 52 in *How to Teach Spelling*.

# /ô/—Spelled *au* and *aw*

Read, copy, and learn.

1. Use au at the beginning or in the middle of a word unless the /ô/ sound is followed by a single n or l; then use aw.

_______________

_______________

_______________

| | | |
|---|---|---|
| pause ________ | dawn ________ | crawl ________ |
| because ________ | lawn ________ | shawl ________ |
| saucer ________ | drawn ________ | brawl ________ |
| laundry ________ | pawn ________ | scrawl ________ |

2. Use aw at the end of a word for the /ô/ sound.

_______________

_______________

saw ________ jaw ________ draw ________ straw ________

Read, copy, and learn the exceptions.

| | | |
|---|---|---|
| awe ________ | awkward ________ | haul ________ |
| awful ________ | squawk ________ | Paul ________ |
| hawk ________ | hawthorn ________ | |
| awning ________ | lawyer ________ | |

Fill in the blanks with either *au* or *aw*. Then read the words. Place a check in front of the words that are exceptions to the generalizations.

| | | | |
|---|---|---|---|
| r____ | v____lt | b____l | f____lt |
| ____l | sh____l | h____k | ____to |
| f____cet | cl____ | ____kward | s____ce |
| l____n | br____l | sp____n | g____dy |
| scr____l | squ____k | t____t | ____thor |
| bec____se | h____l | s____ | str____ |
| l____ndry | s____sage | l____nch | p____se |
| y____n | ____ning | ____tumn | dr____n |
| l____ | ____ful | fl____ | P____l |
| s____nter | h____nt | g____nt | appl____d |

**Use a separate sheet of paper to write the words, phrases, and sentences dictated by your teacher. This dictation will check your ability to spell words with *au* and *aw*.[1]**

[1] Dictate words, phrases, and sentences from the lists on pages 53, 54, and 55 in *How to Teach Spelling*.

# /ôt/—Spelled *aught* and *ought*

**Read, copy, and learn.**

The /ôt/ sound is spelled aught or ought.

______________________________________________

**Read, copy, and learn this nonsense sentence that contains the six *aught* words.**

The farmer caught his haughty, naughty daughter and taught her not to slaughter animals.

______________________________________________

______________________________________________

______________________________________________

**Read, copy, and learn the seven *ought* words.**

ought ____________ sought ____________

bought ____________ thought ____________

brought ____________ wrought ____________

fought ____________

As you read the story, fill in the blanks with either *aught* or *ought.* Then read the story again.

The Birthday Present

One day the mail carrier br__ought__ a package to Mrs. Brown's house. Her d__________er Penny opened the door. It was a package for her sister Betty. "Oh," she th__________, "I __________ to wait until Betty's birthday to see what it is." Just then she c__________ sight of her mother, and the n__________y little girl hid the large parcel that the mail carrier had br__________.

Betty always looked forward to the special presents that her aunt from Boston b__________ for her. But on this birthday there was no package from Aunt Toby. Little did she know that the new game her n__________y sister Penny was playing __________ to have been hers. Penny t__________ Betty to play her new game but Betty began to play so well that Penny would get sl__________ered when she played against her sister. Penny began to cry and picked a fight with Betty. They f__________ and f__________. When their mother s__________ an explanation for the appearance of this new game, which caused the fight, the truth came out. N__________y little Penny th__________ it was unfair for her sister to have a birthday and get presents. She the th__________ that she __________ to have a birthday, too. Her mother t__________ her that birthdays come only once a year and made her return the game to Betty. Mother said she __________ to apologize to Betty, and she whispered in Penny's ear that she had already b__________ a special present for her birthday, which wasn't very far off.

**Use a separate sheet of paper to write the phrases dictated by your teacher. This dictation will check your ability to spell words with *aught* and *ought.*[1]**

[1] Dictate phrases from the list on page 56 in *How to Teach Spelling.*

# Plurals

Read, copy, and learn.

Plural means "more than one."

______________________________

Plurals are formed by adding s or es to singular words.

______________________________

______________________________

When the end sound of the base word comes through your teeth, add es. If the end sound of the base word does not come through your teeth, add only s.

______________________________

______________________________

______________________________

If the base word ends in silent e, add only s.

______________________________

Write the plural of these words.

| | | | |
|---|---|---|---|
| book | __________ | stitch | __________ |
| sail | __________ | bridge | __________ |
| box | __________ | show | __________ |
| gas | __________ | case | __________ |
| brush | __________ | bike | __________ |
| church | __________ | paper | __________ |
| dress | __________ | carpet | __________ |

**Use a separate sheet of paper to write the sentences dictated by your teacher. This dictation will check your ability to spell plural words.**[1]

[1] Dictate sentences from the list on pages 57 and 58 in *How to Teach Spelling*.

# Contractions

**Read, copy, and learn.**

A contraction is one word made from two words. One or more letters are left out when combining the two words, and those letters that are left out are replaced with an apostrophe (').

**Read and learn. Copy the contractions.**

| | | | | | | | |
|---|---|---|---|---|---|---|---|
| he's | = | he is | he's | hadn't | = | had not | |
| she's | = | she is | | I've | = | I have | |
| I'm | = | I am | | he'll | = | he will | |
| I'd | = | I would | | she'll | = | she will | |
| I'll | = | I will | | you'll | = | you will | |
| it's | = | it is | | we'll | = | we will | |
| isn't | = | is not | | here's | = | here is | |
| don't | = | do not | | that's | = | that is | |
| didn't | = | did not | | what's | = | what is | |
| doesn't | = | does not | | let's | = | let us | |
| can't | = | cannot | | who's | = | who is | |
| won't | = | will not | | you're | = | you are | |
| aren't | = | are not | | you've | = | you have | |
| wasn't | = | was not | | there's | = | there is | |
| weren't | = | were not | | they're | = | they are | |
| hasn't | = | has not | | they've | = | they have | |
| haven't | = | have not | | they'll | = | they will | |

## Contractions (continued)

| | | | |
|---|---|---|---|
| we're | = | we are | ____ |
| we've | = | we have | ____ |
| couldn't | = | could not | ____ |
| wouldn't | = | would not | ____ |
| shouldn't | = | should not | ____ |

Write the contractions for these words.

| | | | |
|---|---|---|---|
| has not | hasn't | she is | ____ |
| he is | ____ | I will | ____ |
| is not | ____ | it is | ____ |
| did not | ____ | do not | ____ |
| cannot | ____ | had not | ____ |
| you will | ____ | I am | ____ |
| who is | ____ | does not | ____ |
| you have | ____ | we will | ____ |
| are not | ____ | let us | ____ |
| was not | ____ | you are | ____ |
| have not | ____ | will not | ____ |
| I have | ____ | were not | ____ |
| she will | ____ | he will | ____ |
| here is | ____ | that is | ____ |
| what is | ____ | I would | ____ |

**Use a separate sheet of paper to write the sentences dictated by your teacher. This dictation will check your ability to spell contractions.**[1]

[1] Dictate sentences from the list on pages 59, 60, and 61 in *How to Teach Spelling*.

# The Doubling Rule (The 1-1-1 Rule)

**Read, copy, and learn.**

If a one-syllable base word ends in one consonant with one vowel before it, you must double the final consonant of the base word when adding a suffix that begins with a vowel. Do not double the final consonant if the suffix begins with a consonant.

| | | | | | | | | | | | | | |
|---|---|---|---|---|---|---|---|---|---|---|---|---|---|
| mad | + | est | = | maddest | | thin | + | ed | = | thinned |
| mad | + | er | = | madder | | thin | + | ing | = | thinning |
| mad | + | ly | = | madly | | thin | + | ly | = | thinly |
| mad | + | ness | = | madness | | thin | + | ness | = | thinness |

Never double the final letters w, x, and y.

| | | | | |
|---|---|---|---|---|
| snow | + | ed | = | snowed |
| box | + | ing | = | boxing |
| play | + | er | = | player |

# The Doubling Rule (continued)

*Exercise 1*

Join the base word and suffix to make a new word.

| Base Word | | Suffix | | New Word |
|---|---|---|---|---|
| mad | + | est | = | maddest |
| mad | + | ness | = | ______ |
| dim | + | ly | = | ______ |
| dim | + | ing | = | ______ |
| stop | + | ed | = | ______ |
| glad | + | ly | = | ______ |
| ship | + | ing | = | ______ |
| ship | + | ment | = | ______ |
| wit | + | y | = | ______ |
| rot | + | en | = | ______ |
| split | + | ing | = | ______ |
| step | + | ed | = | ______ |
| fail | + | ing | = | ______ |
| drag | + | ed | = | ______ |
| scrub | + | ing | = | ______ |
| bad | + | ly | = | ______ |
| spoil | + | ing | = | ______ |
| fog | + | y | = | ______ |
| weed | + | ed | = | ______ |
| snow | + | ing | = | ______ |
| quiz | + | ed | = | ______ |
| red | + | ness | = | ______ |

*Exercise 2*

Write the base word and the suffix for the following words.

| | Base Word | Suffix | | Base Word | Suffix |
|---|---|---|---|---|---|
| baggy | bag | y | quizzing | | |
| fanning | | | scrubbed | | |
| stooping | | | madly | | |
| getting | | | madder | | |
| bigger | | | hugged | | |
| trimmed | | | jogging | | |
| dimly | | | pinned | | |
| shipment | | | bigness | | |
| bitten | | | tanned | | |
| boxing | | | reddish | | |
| hotter | | | fitful | | |
| thinness | | | gritty | | |
| deeper | | | bending | | |

**Use a separate sheet of paper to write the words, phrases, and sentences dictated by your teacher. This dictation will check your ability to use the Doubling Rule.**[1]

[1] Dictate words, phrases, and sentences from the lists on pages 63, 64, and 65 in *How to Teach Spelling*.

# Words That End in *ain*

Read, copy, and learn.

The /ĭn/ or /ĕn/ sound at the end of some words is spelled ain.

______________________________________________

______________________________________________

Read, copy, and learn.

| | | | |
|---|---|---|---|
| bargain | ____________ | fountain | ____________ |
| captain | ____________ | mountain | ____________ |
| chaplain | ____________ | villain | ____________ |
| certain | ____________ | Great Britain | ____________ |
| curtain | ____________ | again | ____________ |
| | | against | ____________ |

Use a separate sheet of paper. Write six original sentences. Use as many words ending in *ain* as you can.

**Use a separate sheet of paper to write the phrases and sentences dictated by your teacher. This dictation will check your ability to spell words that end in *ain*.**[1]

[1] Dictate phrases and sentences from the lists on page 66 in *How to Teach Spelling*.

# The Silent-*e* Rule

Read, copy, and learn.

When a word ends in silent e:

1. Drop the e before adding a suffix that begins with a vowel.
   like + able = likable
2. Keep the e before adding a suffix that begins with a consonant.
   like + ness = likeness

____________________

1. ____________________

____________________

____________________

2. ____________________

____________________

____________________

Join the base word and suffix to make a new word.

| Base Word | | Suffix | | New Word |
|---|---|---|---|---|
| care | + | ing | = | __________ |
| care | + | ful | = | __________ |
| use | + | ed | = | __________ |
| use | + | ing | = | __________ |
| use | + | less | = | __________ |
| move | + | ment | = | __________ |
| fame | + | ous | = | __________ |
| shade | + | y | = | __________ |
| loose | + | en | = | __________ |
| nerve | + | ous | = | __________ |
| excite | + | ment | = | __________ |

## Exceptions to the Silent-*e* Rule

Read, copy, and learn.

1. Some words DROP the silent e before a suffix that begins with a consonant.

______________________________

______________________________

Read, copy, and memorize this nonsense sentence. It contains the words that are exceptions.

Truly the ninth argument is wholly awful,[1] but the judgment and acknowledgment are duly accepted as truth.

______________________________

______________________________

______________________________

Read, copy, and learn.[2]

2. Some words KEEP the silent e before a suffix that begins with a vowel. When you add the suffixes -able and -ous to words with a c or g before a final silent e, keep the silent e to keep the c and g soft.

| | | | |
|---|---|---|---|
| noticeable | serviceable | traceable | peaceable |
| pronounceable | enforceable | courageous | outrageous |
| advantageous | changeable | chargeable | manageable |
| marriageable | | | |

2. ______________________________

______________________________

______________________________

______________________________

______________________________

______________________________

[1]Adapted from Mildred B. Plunkett, *A Spelling Workbook Emphasizing Rules and Generalizations for Corrective Drill* (Cambridge, MA: Educators Publishing Service, Inc.), page 46.

[2]Refer to Teacher's Key for grade level recommendations.

3. Some words keep the silent e to preserve their identity.

| dyeing (dyed) | canoeing | hoeing | mileage |
|---|---|---|---|
| singeing | shoeing | toeing | acreage |
| tingeing | | | |

3.

4. The following three words that end in silent e change their spelling when you add the suffix -ing. They do not follow any rule. Simply memorize them.

| | | | | | Past Tense |
|---|---|---|---|---|---|
| die | + | ing | = | dying | died |
| tie | + | ing | = | tying | tied |
| lie | + | ing | = | lying | lied |

4.

Use a separate sheet of paper. Write five original sentences using as many words that are exceptions to the Silent-*e* Rule as you can.

# The Silent-*e* Rule (continued)

*Exercise 1*

Write the base word and the suffix for the following words.

| | Base Word | Suffix |
|---|---|---|
| shiny | ____________ | ________ |
| likeness | ____________ | ________ |
| hopeful | ____________ | ________ |
| grimy | ____________ | ________ |
| sloping | ____________ | ________ |
| skater | ____________ | ________ |
| pavement | ____________ | ________ |
| paving | ____________ | ________ |
| scared | ____________ | ________ |
| waved | ____________ | ________ |
| grating | ____________ | ________ |
| blamed | ____________ | ________ |
| surely | ____________ | ________ |
| draped | ____________ | ________ |
| dining | ____________ | ________ |
| safer | ____________ | ________ |
| giving | ____________ | ________ |
| truly | ____________ | ________ |
| dancing | ____________ | ________ |
| largely | ____________ | ________ |
| riding | ____________ | ________ |
| sliding | ____________ | ________ |

*Exercise 2*

**Join the base word and suffix to make a new word. Circle the exceptions to the Silent-*e* Rule.**

Remember: When you add the suffixes *-able* and *-ous* to words ending with a soft *c* or *g* sound, you do not drop the silent *e* at the end of the word. Example: *notice + able = noticeable.*

| Base Word | | Suffix | | New Word |
|---|---|---|---|---|
| peace | + | able | = | ________________ |
| pronounce | + | able | = | ________________ |
| courage | + | ous | = | ________________ |
| value | + | able | = | ________________ |
| marriage | + | able | = | ________________ |
| advantage | + | ous | = | ________________ |
| trace | + | able | = | ________________ |
| enforce | + | able | = | ________________ |
| outrage | + | ous | = | ________________ |
| service | + | able | = | ________________ |
| change | + | able | = | ________________ |
| fame | + | ous | = | ________________ |
| notice | + | able | = | ________________ |
| love | + | able | = | ________________ |
| manage | + | able | = | ________________ |
| sale | + | able | = | ________________ |
| charge | + | able | = | ________________ |

**Use a separate sheet of paper to write the words, phrases, and sentences dictated by your teacher. This dictation will check your ability to use the Silent-e Rule.**[1]

[1] Dictate words, phrases, and sentences from the lists on pages 68, 69, 70, 71, and 72 in *How to Teach Spelling*.

## Review of Doubling Rule and Silent-*e* Rule

Join the base word and suffix to make a new word.

| Base Word | | Suffix | | New Word |
|---|---|---|---|---|
| rude | + | ly | = | ____________ |
| quit | + | er | = | ____________ |
| true | + | ly | = | ____________ |
| complete | + | ing | = | ____________ |
| use | + | ing | = | ____________ |
| clap | + | ed | = | ____________ |
| skin | + | y | = | ____________ |
| sure | + | ly | = | ____________ |
| change | + | able | = | ____________ |
| move | + | able | = | ____________ |
| share | + | ing | = | ____________ |
| argue | + | ment | = | ____________ |
| like | + | ness | = | ____________ |
| excite | + | ment | = | ____________ |
| scrub | + | ed | = | ____________ |
| quiz | + | ing | = | ____________ |
| lend | + | ing | = | ____________ |
| dine | + | er | = | ____________ |
| improve | + | ment | = | ____________ |
| droop | + | ing | = | ____________ |
| scar | + | ed | = | ____________ |
| safe | + | ly | = | ____________ |
| hope | + | ful | = | ____________ |

## Homophones

**Read, copy, and learn.**

A homophone is a word that sounds the same as another word or words but has a different meaning and is spelled differently.

________________________________________

________________________________________

________________________________________

Read this list of homophones. Then your teacher will tell you which homophones to write in original sentences on a separate sheet of paper. Be sure your sentences tell the meaning of the homophone. Look up in a dictionary the meaning of any word you do not know.

| | | |
|---|---|---|
| air—heir | ate—eight | ball—bawl |
| be—bee | bear—bare | blew—blue |
| break—brake | bury—berry | by—buy |
| capital—capitol | ceiling—sealing | cereal—serial |
| coarse—course | dear—deer | desert—dessert |
| die—dye | due—dew—do | fair—fare |
| feet—feat | flew—flue—flu | flower—flour |
| foul—fowl | four—for | fur—fir |
| groan—grown | guessed—guest | hair—hare |
| hall—haul | heal—heel | heard—herd |
| here—hear | hoarse—horse | hour—our |
| I—eye | kernel—colonel | knew—new |
| knot—not | know—no | lesson—lessen |
| lone—loan | made—maid | mail—male |
| main—mane—Maine | meet—meat | minor—miner |
| night—knight | nose—knows | one—won |

## Homophones (continued)

| | | |
|---|---|---|
| pain—pane | pale—pail | passed—past |
| pause—paws | peak—peek | pear—pair—pare |
| piece—peace | plain—plane | pole—poll |
| presence—presents | principal—principle | rain—reign—rein |
| red—read | right—write | ring—wring |
| road—rode—rowed | roll—role | route—root |
| sale—sail | seen—scene | sees—seas—seize |
| sense—cents | sent—cent—scent | shown—shone |
| so—sew—sow | some—sum | stair—stare |
| stationary—stationery | steak—stake | steel—steal |
| son—sun | straight—strait | tale—tail |
| taught—taut | threw—through | thrown—throne |
| toe—tow | vane—vain—vein | wait—weight |
| waste—waist | way—weigh | wear—ware |
| week—weak | whole—hole | wrote—rote |

## Homophones— Two, To, Too

Read, copy, and learn.

two: 1. a number; one plus one (I have two cats.)
to: 1. a preposition (He ran to school.)
too: 1. also (I am going, too.)
2. more than is needed (I ate too much candy.)

______________________________________________________________________

______________________________________________________________________

______________________________________________________________________

**Fill in the blanks with the correct word (*to, too,* or *two*).**

*Exercise 1*

We want ___to___ play a game. Can more than ________ play? If so, can John play, ________? We were given until ________ o'clock ________ finish our game, but that was ________ much time. We suggested that the teacher choose ________ other boys ________ play next time.

*Exercise 2*

The people wanted ________ travel. They heard that it would be ________ dangerous ________ cross the ________ bridges near the towns they hoped ________ visit. How else could they get ________ these towns? They looked at a map and found ________ other ways ________ go.

**Use a separate sheet of paper to write the sentences dictated by your teacher. This dictation will check your ability to spell the homphones *to, too, and two.*** [1]

## Homophones— There, Their, They're

Read, copy, and learn.

there: 1. a place (Let's meet there.)
2. used in the expression there are (There are the girls.)

their: 1. possessive form of they (Their books are at school.)

they're: 1. a contraction of they are (They're all going home.)

________________________________________

________________________________________

________________________________________

________________________________________

________________________________________

[1] Dictate sentences from the list on pages 73 and 74 in *How to Teach Spelling.*

Fill in the blanks with the correct word (*there, their,* or *they're*).

1. ____________ is a red sweater in the closet.
2. ____________ are four boys in the game.
3. ____________ having a nice vacation.
4. ____________ aunt came to dinner.
5. ____________ coming home to dinner.
6. The tallest tree is over ____________.
7. ____________ aren't many books, so please share.
8. Is your book at ____________ house?
9. ____________ on ____________ way to school.
10. ____________ are not any notebooks in ____________ classroom.
11. ____________ eating ____________ lunch right now.
12. If ____________ at home now, we can go over to ____________ house.
13. ____________ planning to sail ____________ boat ____________ this weekend.
14. ____________ solving the hardest problems in ____________ math books.
15. ____________ brother and Timmy are building ____________ own private tree house over ____________.
16. ____________ thinking up a surprise for ____________ mother.
17. ____________ are two bird's nests hidden in ____________ garden.
18. Sam and Tom saw ____________ teacher in that store over ____________.
19. ____________ the best spellers in ____________ class.

**Use a separate sheet of paper to write the sentences dictated by your teacher. This dictation will check your ability to spell the homophones *there, their,* and *they're.*[1]**

[1] Dictate sentences from the list on pages 75 and 76 in *How to Teach Spelling*.

# Sight Word List 4

Read and copy these words. Learn to spell them.

| | | | |
|---|---|---|---|
| route | ________ | broad | ________ |
| flood | ________ | length | ________ |
| blood | ________ | strength | ________ |
| heart | ________ | special | ________ |
| tongue | ________ | especially | ________ |
| move | ________ | almighty | ________ |
| prove | ________ | altogether | ________ |
| oh | ________ | boulder | ________ |
| owe | ________ | shoulder | ________ |
| soul | ________ | group | ________ |
| usual | ________ | troupe | ________ |
| purpose | ________ | tough | ________ |
| suppose | ________ | rough | ________ |
| half (halves) | ________ ________ | enough | ________ |
| calf (calves) | ________ ________ | dough | ________ |
| wolf (wolves) | ________ ________ | cough | ________ |
| sure | ________ | court | ________ |
| sugar | ________ | course | ________ |
| orange | ________ | coarse | ________ |
| skiing | ________ | though | ________ |
| machine | ________ | through | ________ |
| spirit | ________ | thorough | ________ |
| clothes | ________ | although | ________ |
| material | ________ | | |

**After you know how to spell all the words on Sight Word List 4, use a separate sheet of paper to write the sentences dictated by your teacher.**[1]

[1] Dictate sentences from the list on pages 77 and 78 in *How to Teach Spelling*.

# The Suffixes *-ful* and *-ly*

Read, copy, and learn.

-ful

1. The suffix -ful is spelled with just one l.
2. Add ful to base words without changing them. -ful means "full of." It forms adjectives and, sometimes, nouns.

| | | | | | | | | | |
|---|---|---|---|---|---|---|---|---|---|
| pain | + | ful | = | painful | hand | + | ful | = | handful |

-ly

1. Add ly to base words without changing them.
2. If the base word ends in l, there will be two l's.

| | | | | | | | | | |
|---|---|---|---|---|---|---|---|---|---|
| total | + | ly | = | totally | final | + | ly | = | finally |

3. When adding ly to consonant-le words, drop the le and add ly.

| | | | | | | | | | |
|---|---|---|---|---|---|---|---|---|---|
| simple | + | ly | = | simply | sensible | + | ly | = | sensibly |
| gentle | + | ly | = | gently | probable | + | ly | = | probably |
| double | + | ly | = | doubly | possible | + | ly | = | possibly |
| feeble | + | ly | = | feebly | | | | | |

-<u>ful</u>

1. ______________________________
2. ______________________________
______________________________
______________________________
______________________________

-<u>ly</u>

1. ______________________________
2. ______________________________
______________________________
3. ______________________________
______________________________
______________________________
______________________________
______________________________
______________________________

## The Suffixes *-ful* and *-ly* (continued)

Add *ful* or *ly* to these words to make a new word.

| | | | | |
|---|---|---|---|---|
| total | + | ly | = | ____________ |
| help | + | ful | = | ____________ |
| close | + | ly | = | ____________ |
| large | + | ly | = | ____________ |
| thank | + | ful | = | ____________ |
| general | + | ly | = | ____________ |

Read, copy, and learn.

Both ful and ly can be added to base words without changing them.

______________________________________________

______________________________________________

| | | | | | |
|---|---|---|---|---|---|
| part | ________ | partly | ________ | | |
| glad | ________ | gladly | ________ | | |
| love | ________ | lovely | ________ | | |
| safe | ________ | safely | ________ | | |
| hope | ________ | hopeful | ________ | hopefully | ________ |
| use | ________ | useful | ________ | usefully | ________ |
| care | ________ | careful | ________ | carefully | ________ |
| peace | ________ | peaceful | ________ | peacefully | ________ |
| sorrow | ________ | sorrowful | ________ | sorrowfully | ________ |
| respect | ________ | respectful | ________ | respectfully | ________ |

**Use a separate sheet of paper to write the phrases dictated by your teacher. This dictation will check your ability to spell words that end in *ful* and *ly*.**[1]

[1] Dictate phrases from the list on page 80 in *How to Teach Spelling*.

# /ē/—Spelled *y* and *ey*

Read and learn. Copy the words.

*y* is a common ending for many words in English. It usually says /ē/ at the end of two- and three-syllable words.

| | | |
|---|---|---|
| party ______ | puppy ______ | happy ______ |
| candy ______ | skinny ______ | dirty ______ |

*ey* is a far less common way of spelling the /ē/ sound at the end of words. There are only about forty of these words. The most important are:

| | | |
|---|---|---|
| key ______ | hockey ______ | chimney ______ |
| alley ______ | jockey ______ | medley ______ |
| attorney ______ | jersey ______ | motley ______ |
| donkey ______ | valley ______ | kidney ______ |
| monkey ______ | volley ______ | journey ______ |
| money ______ | galley ______ | parsley ______ |
| honey ______ | turkey ______ | whiskey ______ |

The few common words that end in *ey* with *ey* saying /ā/ are:

| | | |
|---|---|---|
| they ______ | survey ______ | obey ______ |
| hey ______ | convey ______ | prey ______ |

Use a separate sheet of paper. Write nine original sentences using as many words that end in *ey* as you can.

**Use a separate sheet of paper to write the phrases dictated by your teacher. This dictation will check your ability to spell words that end in *y* and *ey*.[1]**

[1] Dictate phrases from the list on page 81 in *How to Teach Spelling*.

# The *Y* Rule

Read, copy, and learn.

1. If the letter before a final y is a vowel, the y doesn't change when you add a suffix.
   play      played      playing      playful

2. If the letter before a final y is a consonant, the y changes to i when you add a suffix, except when the suffix begins with an i.
   carry      carried      carrier      carrying

Read, copy, and learn some exceptions to the *Y* Rule.

day + ly = daily

gay + ly = gaily

pay + ed = paid

say + ed = said

lay + ed = laid

mislay + ed = mislaid

slay becomes slain

Read, copy, and learn some more exceptions to the *Y* Rule.

shy + ly = shyly

dry + ly = dryly

sly + ly = slyly

spry + ly = spryly

shy + ness = shyness

dry + ness = dryness

sly + ness = slyness

spry + ness = spryness

*Exercise 1*

Add the suffix to the base word to make a new word.

| Base Word | | Suffix | | New Word |
|---|---|---|---|---|
| carry | + | ed | = | ____________ |
| busy | + | er | = | ____________ |
| carry | + | er | = | ____________ |
| busy | + | ness | = | ____________ |
| carry | + | ing | = | ____________ |
| beauty | + | ful | = | ____________ |
| hurry | + | ed | = | ____________ |
| fly | + | ing | = | ____________ |
| rely | + | ing | = | ____________ |
| fly | + | es | = | ____________ |
| rely | + | ed | = | ____________ |
| rely | + | able | = | ____________ |
| study | + | ous | = | ____________ |
| copy | + | ist | = | ____________ |
| lovely | + | ness | = | ____________ |
| happy | + | ness | = | ____________ |
| greedy | + | er | = | ____________ |
| merry | + | est | = | ____________ |
| joy | + | ful | = | ____________ |
| duty | + | ful | = | ____________ |
| delay | + | ing | = | ____________ |
| day | + | ly | = | ____________ |
| lay | + | ed | = | ____________ |

# The *Y* Rule (continued)

*Exercise 2*

Write the base word and the suffix for the following words.

| | Base Word | Suffix |
|---|---|---|
| dried | ______________ | _________ |
| carrier | ______________ | _________ |
| spying | ______________ | _________ |
| busier | ______________ | _________ |
| payment | ______________ | _________ |
| beautiful | ______________ | _________ |
| annoyed | ______________ | _________ |
| reliable | ______________ | _________ |
| appliance | ______________ | _________ |
| enjoyment | ______________ | _________ |
| enjoyed | ______________ | _________ |
| studying | ______________ | _________ |
| glorious | ______________ | _________ |
| supplied | ______________ | _________ |
| studious | ______________ | _________ |
| flying | ______________ | _________ |
| flies | ______________ | _________ |
| laziest | ______________ | _________ |
| joyful | ______________ | _________ |
| prettiest | ______________ | _________ |
| luckiest | ______________ | _________ |
| loneliness | ______________ | _________ |

Read, copy, and learn these words.

| | | | | |
|---|---|---|---|---|
| twenty | — | twentieth | ____________ | ____________ |
| thirty | — | thirtieth | ____________ | ____________ |
| forty | — | fortieth | ____________ | ____________ |
| fifty | — | fiftieth | ____________ | ____________ |
| sixty | — | sixtieth | ____________ | ____________ |
| seventy | — | seventieth | ____________ | ____________ |
| eighty | — | eightieth | ____________ | ____________ |
| ninety | — | ninetieth | ____________ | ____________ |

**Use a separate sheet of paper to write the words, phrases, and sentences dictated by your teacher. This dictation will check your ability to spell words that follow and are exceptions to the *Y* Rule.**[1]

[1] Dictate words, phrases, and sentences from the lists on pages 83, 84, and 85 in *How to Teach Spelling*.

# Rules Poster

Color this poster. Study it. You may cut it out of this book and put it above your desk to remind you of some spelling rules.

DOUBLE DROP CHANGE

**111 Words**

DOUBLE the final consonant if the suffix begins with a Vowel

EXAMPLE: Sad, sadder, sadness

(do not double if the suffix begins with a consonant)

**Silent-e Words**

DROP the final e if the suffix begins with a Vowel

EXAMPLE: Name, naming, nameless

(Keep the e if the suffix begins with a consonant)

**Words ending in y**

CHANGE the y to i if there is a Consonant before the y

EXAMPLE: Cry, cried

except if the suffix begins with an i

EXAMPLE: cry, crying

(Keep the y if a vowel comes before the y)

EXAMPLE: play, played

## Review of Doubling Rule, Silent-*e* Rule, and *Y* Rule

Add the suffix to the base word to make a new word; then state which rule you are using: 1 = Doubling Rule
2 = Silent-*e* Rule
3 = *Y* Rule

| Base Word | | Suffix | | New Word | Rule |
|---|---|---|---|---|---|
| happy | + | ness | = | happiness | 3 |
| dim | + | ing | = | | |
| like | + | able | = | | |
| enjoy | + | able | = | | |
| nerve | + | ous | = | | |
| like | + | ness | = | | |
| trip | + | ed | = | | |
| jump | + | ing | = | | |
| trade | + | ing | = | | |
| cram | + | ed | = | | |
| sparkle | + | ing | = | | |
| scare | + | ed | = | | |
| obey | + | ed | = | | |
| scar | + | ed | = | | |
| merry | + | ly | = | | |
| wise | + | ly | = | | |
| wit | + | y | = | | |
| spoke | + | en | = | | |
| dim | + | ly | = | | |

# *tion* and *sion*

Read, copy, and learn everything on this page.

1. The sound /shŭn/ is spelled two ways: tion and sion. If you aren't sure which to use, try tion; tion is the more commonly used form.
2. If the original word ends in ss, the /shŭn/ sound is always spelled sion. Memorize the spelling of these words:

| | | |
|---|---|---|
| confess—confession | impress—impression | progress—progression |
| depress—depression | possess—possession | recess—recession |
| discuss—discussion | process—procession | regress—regression |
| express—expression | profess—profession | success—succession |

3. /shŭn/ is spelled cion in two words: coercion, suspicion.
4. /chŭn/ is spelled tion in these few words: question, mention, attention, contention.
5. /chŭn/ is spelled sion in words such as: comprehension, expansion, extension, apprehension, suspension.
6. If you hear /zhŭn/ in a word, it can only be spelled sion: television, explosion, confusion.
7. /shŭn/ is spelled xion in the word complexion.

Which end sounds do you hear in these words? Fill in the blanks with either /shŭn/, /chŭn/, or /zhŭn/.

| | | | |
|---|---|---|---|
| question | /chŭn/ | objection | ______ |
| emotion | ______ | impression | ______ |
| attention | ______ | conclusion | ______ |
| addition | ______ | television | ______ |
| exclusion | ______ | composition | ______ |
| fusion | ______ | confession | ______ |
| occasion | ______ | recession | ______ |
| attraction | ______ | version | ______ |
| ambition | ______ | discussion | ______ |
| invasion | ______ | collection | ______ |
| expression | ______ | succession | ______ |
| possession | ______ | separation | ______ |
| commission | ______ | provision | ______ |
| mention | ______ | profession | ______ |

Write five original sentences using as many of the words listed as you can.

1. ______________________________

______________________________

2. ______________________________

______________________________

3. ______________________________

______________________________

4. ______________________________

______________________________

5. ______________________________

______________________________

## *-tion* and *-sion* (continued)

Fill in the blanks with *tion* or *sion* and write the number of the reason you chose either *tion* or *sion.*

The reason for choosing a particular ending should be one of the following:

1. The original word ends in *ss* . . . so we use *sion.*
2. The ending says /shŭn/ . . . so we use *tion.*
3. The ending says /chŭn/ . . . so we use *tion.*
4. The ending says /zhŭn/ . . . so we use *sion.*

Remember: /shŭn/ is spelled *tion* as in *station.*
/shŭn/ is spelled *sion* if the word to which it is added ends in *ss.*
/chŭn/ is spelled *tion* as in *question.*
/zhŭn/ is spelled *sion* as in *television.*

| Add *tion* or *sion* | Reason | Add *tion* or *sion* | Reason |
|---|---|---|---|
| ac tion | 2 | explo______ | ______ |
| na______ | ______ | sta______ | ______ |
| mo______ | ______ | ques______ | ______ |
| vi______ | ______ | expres______ | ______ |
| divi______ | ______ | atten______ | ______ |
| men______ | ______ | diver______ | ______ |
| discus______ | ______ | impres______ | ______ |
| inva______ | ______ | subtrac______ | ______ |
| confes______ | ______ | posses______ | ______ |
| profes______ | ______ | conclu______ | ______ |
| no______ | ______ | protec______ | ______ |
| confu______ | ______ | proces______ | ______ |

**Use a separate sheet of paper to write the words, phrases, and sentences dictated by your teacher. This dictation will check your ability to spell words that end with *tion* and *sion.*[1]**

[1] Dictate words, phrases, and sentences from the lists on pages 88, 89, and 90 in *How to Teach Spelling.*

# The *i*-before-*e* Generalization

Read, copy, and learn. Copy

Put i before e ____________________

Except after c ____________________

Or when sounded like /ā/ ____________________

As in neighbor and weigh. ____________________

Read, copy, and learn the first group of words. Look up the meaning of any word you do not know.

Put *i* before e

1. chief ________________
   handkerchief ________________
   mischief ________________
   mischievous ________________
   thief ________________
   brief ________________
   grief ________________
   belief ________________
   relief ________________
   grieve ________________
   believe ________________
   relieve ________________
   achieve ________________
   retrieve ________________
   reprieve ________________

Do not move on to word groups 2, 3, and 4 until you can write group 1 from memory on a separate sheet of paper.

Read, copy, and learn.

2. niece ____________
   piece ____________
   pierce ____________
   fierce ____________
3. field ____________
   shield ____________
   wield ____________
   yield ____________
4. pier ____________
   tier ____________
   cashier ____________
   frontier ____________

# The *i*-before-*e* Generalization (continued)

After you have learned to spell and to write from memory all the words in groups 1, 2, 3, and 4, read, copy, and learn the words in groups 5 and 6. Notice that in group 6, *ie* does not have the sound of /ē/.

| | | | |
|---|---|---|---|
| 5. | fiend ____________ | 6. | friend ____________ |
| | priest ____________ | | sieve ____________ |
| | shriek ____________ | | view ____________ |
| | siege ____________ | | review ____________ |
| | besiege ____________ | | interview ____________ |
| | hygiene ____________ | | |

Read, copy, and learn.

Except after *c*

| | | | |
|---|---|---|---|
| 1. | ceiling ____________ | 2. | conceit ____________ |
| | receipt ____________ | | deceit ____________ |
| | receive ____________ | | conceive ____________ |
| | | | deceive ____________ |
| | | | perceive ____________ |

Or when sounded like /ā/

| | | | | |
|---|---|---|---|---|
| 1. | eight ________ | 3. | vein ________ | their ________ |
| | weight ________ | | veil ________ | beige ________ |
| | freight ________ | | skein ________ | heir ________ |
| 2. | weigh ________ | | rein ________ | heiress ________ |
| | sleigh ________ | | reindeer ________ | [1]feign ________ |
| | neigh ________ | | reign ________ | [1]deign ________ |
| | neighbor ________ | | | [1]inveigle ________ |

[1] Refer to Teacher's Key for grade level recommendations.

## Exceptions to the *i*-before-*e* Generalization

Read, copy, and learn this nonsense sentence, which contains six of the exceptions spelled *ei*.

| Neither | leisured | foreigner | seized | the weird height.[1] |
|---|---|---|---|---|
| (either) | (leisure) | (foreign) | (seize) | |

______________________________________________

______________________________________________

More exceptions spelled with *ei* to read, copy, and learn.[2] Look up the meaning of any words you do not know.

| | | | | | |
|---|---|---|---|---|---|
| forfeit | ____________ | caffeine | ____________ | sheik | ____________ |
| counterfeit | ____________ | protein | ____________ | heifer | ____________ |
| surfeit | ____________ | sovereign | ____________ | sleight | ____________ |

More exceptions to read, copy, and learn. In these exceptions, *ie* comes after *c*.

| (*ci* stays /sh/ in these words) | | (*fici* says /fish/ in these words) | |
|---|---|---|---|
| ancient | ________________ | efficient | ________________ |
| species | ________________ | sufficient | ________________ |
| glacier | ________________ | deficient | ________________ |
| conscience | ________________ | proficient | ________________ |

Write two original sentences using some of the exceptions taken from the nonsense sentence.

______________________________________________

______________________________________________

______________________________________________

______________________________________________

______________________________________________

______________________________________________

[1] Mildred B. Plunkett, *A Spelling Workbook for Corrective Drill for Elementary Grades* (Cambridge, MA: Educators Publishing Service, Inc.), page 66.

[2] Refer to Teacher's Key for grade level recommendations.

Fill in the blanks with either *ie* or *ei*. Then read the words.

| *Exercise 1* | | *Exercise 2* | |
|---|---|---|---|
| b_ei_ge | gr____ve | v____l | v____n |
| ch____f | s____ve | v____w | br____f |
| c____ling | retr____ve | gr____f | w____ld |
| n____ce | r____ndeer | f____rce | cash____r |
| f____ld | p____rce | n____ghbor | fr____nd |
| th____r | w____ght | w____gh | h____ght |
| p____r | shr____k | y____ld | t____r |
| f____nd | fr____ght | front____r | dec____ve |
| rec____pt | ach____ve | s____ge | rel____f |
| th____f | bel____f | sl____gh | w____rd |
| misch____f | n____ther | rev____w | bel____ve |
| p____ce | r____gn | bes____ge | l____sure |
| sh____ld | s____ze | rec____ve | conc____t |

*Exercise 3*[1]

| | | | |
|---|---|---|---|
| n____ther | profic____nt | caff____ne | conc____ve |
| perc____ve | prot____n | suffic____nt | for____gner |
| forf____t | dec____t | h____fer | spec____s |
| effic____nt | anc____nt | ____ther | ____ght |
| pr____st | consc____nce | counterf____t | glac____r |
| h____ght | defic____nt | surf____t | sl____ght |

**Use a separate sheet of paper to write the phrases and sentences dictated by your teacher. This dictation will check your ability to spell words with *ie* and *ei*.**[2]

[1] Refer to Teacher's Key for grade level recommendations.

[2] Dictate phrases and sentences from the lists on pages 93, 94, and 95 in *How to Teach Spelling*.

# More Plurals

Review: Plural means "more than one." Plurals are formed by adding *s* or *es*. When the end sound of the base word comes through your teeth, add *es*. If it does not come through your teeth, add *s*. If the base word ends in silent *e*, add *s*.

wall—walls | box—boxes | face—faces

**Read. Copy and learn the words.**

1. Words ending in *y* follow the *Y* Rule.
   a. Words ending in *y* preceded by a vowel become plural by adding *s*.

      boy—boys ________________ play—plays ________________

   b. Words ending in *y* preceded by a consonant become plural by changing the *y* to *i* and adding *es*.

      copy—copies ________________ cry—cries ________________

2. Words ending in *f* or *fe*.
   a. Words ending in *f* or *fe* usually become plural by adding *s*.

      chief ________________ chiefs ________________

      roof ________________ roofs ________________

      safe ________________ safes ________________

   b. Some words ending in *f* or *fe* become plural by changing the *f* or *fe* to *v* and adding *es*.

      calf ________________ calves ________________

      elf ________________ elves ________________

      half ________________ halves ________________

      knife ________________ knives ________________

      leaf ________________ leaves ________________

      life ________________ lives ________________

      loaf ________________ loaves ________________

      self ________________ selves ________________

      scarf ________________ scarves ________________

# More Plurals (continued)

shelf ______________ shelves ________________

thief ______________ thieves ________________

wharf ______________ wharves ________________

wife ______________ wives ________________

wolf ______________ wolves ________________

3. Words ending in *o*.
   a. Words ending in *o* preceded by a vowel become plural by adding *s*.

   embryo ______________ embryos ________________

   radio ______________ radios ________________

   ratio ______________ ratios ________________

   rodeo ______________ rodeos ________________

   shampoo ______________ shampoos ________________

   studio ______________ studios ________________

   b. Most words ending in *o* preceded by a consonant become plural by adding *es*.

   buffalo ______________ buffaloes ________________

   hero ______________ heroes ________________

   potato ______________ potatoes ________________

   tomato ______________ tomatoes ________________

   Common exceptions:

   dynamo ______________ dynamos ________________

   ditto ______________ dittos ________________

   photo ______________ photos ________________

   pro ______________ pros ________________

   silo ______________ silos ________________

c. Words of Spanish origin, Italian musical terms, and proper names ending in *o* become plural by adding *s*.

| | |
|---|---|
| burro ____________ | burros ____________ |
| bronco ____________ | broncos ____________ |
| lasso ____________ | lassos ____________ |
| poncho ____________ | ponchos ____________ |
| pueblo ____________ | pueblos ____________ |
| sombrero ____________ | sombreros ____________ |
| soprano ____________ | sopranos ____________ |
| contralto ____________ | contraltos ____________ |
| piano ____________ | pianos ____________ |
| cello ____________ | cellos ____________ |
| libretto ____________ | librettos ____________ |
| solo ____________ | solos ____________ |
| Romeo ____________ | Romeos ____________ |
| Eskimo ____________ | Eskimos ____________ |
| Filipino ____________ | Filipinos ____________ |

4. Letters and numbers
   a. Letters, numbers, and signs become plural by adding *'s*.

| | | | |
|---|---|---|---|
| *x*'s ______ | 7's ______ | 1980's______ | +'s ______ |
| *b*'s ______ | 10's ______ | 1490's______ | −'s ______ |

5. Irregular plurals
   a. Some words form their plurals irregularly.

| | |
|---|---|
| child ____________ | children ____________ |
| man ____________ | men ____________ |
| woman ____________ | women ____________ |
| ox ____________ | oxen ____________ |
| mouse ____________ | mice ____________ |

## More Plurals (continued)

| | |
|---|---|
| louse ______ | lice ______ |
| goose ______ | geese ______ |
| foot ______ | feet ______ |
| tooth ______ | teeth ______ |

6. Singular and plural spellings that are the same
   a. Some words are the same in both the singular and the plural.

| | |
|---|---|
| sheep ______ | species ______ |
| deer ______ | Chinese ______ |
| moose ______ | Japanese ______ |
| trout ______ | scissors ______ |
| salmon ______ | trousers ______ |
| grapefruit ______ | |

Write the plural of the following words.

*Exercise 1*

| Singular | Plural | Singular | Plural |
|---|---|---|---|
| fly | flies | self | ______ |
| bench | ______ | shampoo | ______ |
| puppy | ______ | safe | ______ |
| tray | ______ | wolf | ______ |
| key | ______ | scarf | ______ |
| blotter | ______ | tomato | ______ |
| ring | ______ | chief | ______ |
| sheep | ______ | leaf | ______ |
| half | ______ | radio | ______ |
| judge | ______ | donkey | ______ |

*Exercise 2*

| Singular | Plural |
|---|---|
| spy | |
| victory | |
| fox | |
| child | |
| tooth | |
| sound | |
| shelf | |
| knife | |
| umbrella | |
| president | |
| porch | |
| million | |
| nation | |
| pony | |
| potato | |
| loaf | |
| buffalo | |
| alto | |
| ox | |
| wife | |
| salmon | |
| wharf | |
| life | |
| studio | |
| piano | |
| dynamo | |

*Exercise 3*

| Singular | Plural |
|---|---|
| country | |
| frame | |
| photo | |
| lunch | |
| hobby | |
| train | |
| holiday | |
| bridge | |
| couple | |
| smile | |
| calf | |
| rodeo | |
| brush | |
| glass | |
| deer | |
| ditto | |
| 1900 | |
| man | |
| woman | |
| pro | |
| solo | |
| mouse | |
| moose | |
| trout | |
| species | |
| louse | |

# Possessive Words

Read, copy, and learn.

Possessive words show ownership or relationship.

1. Singular possessive
   a. Singular words become possessive by adding 's.
      baby's crib   child's tray   boss's office   princess's crown

1.

2. Plural possessive
   a. Plural words ending in s add only an apostrophe.
      babies' toys   princesses' crowns
   b. Other plural words become possessive by adding 's.
      children's room   mice's tracks

2.

3. Possessive personal pronouns
   a. Possessive personal pronouns do not need an apostrophe.
      its   his   hers   ours   yours   theirs

3.

Write each of the following words in the correct column.

| | | | |
|---|---|---|---|
| class's | merchant's | man's | actress's |
| thief's | glasses' | apple's | heroes' |
| jockey's | thieves' | life's | Eskimos' |
| wives' | fairy's | princess's | students' |
| priest's | men's | radios' | student's |
| friend's | sailors' | babies' | Davises' |
| children's | fairies' | Davis's | classes' |

| Singular Possessive Words | | Plural Possessive Words | |
|---|---|---|---|
| Class's | | | |
| | | | |
| | | | |
| | | | |
| | | | |
| | | | |
| | | | |

Use a separate sheet of paper. Write ten original sentences. Use as many possessive words as you can.

# Silent Letters

Many words contain letters that are not pronounced. They may have been pronounced at one time, but our language has changed through usage. Through your reading you are probably familiar with many of these words.

Read. Copy and learn the words.

*b* is not sounded in these words:
doubt, debt, comb, dumb, thumb, tomb, lamb, climb, crumb, numb, plumber, bomb.

__________ __________ __________ __________

__________ __________ __________ __________

__________ __________ __________ __________

*c* is not sounded in these words:
scene, scent, science, scissors, scythe.

__________ __________ __________ __________

__________

*g* is not sounded in these words:
gnat, gnash, gnarl, gnaw, gnome, sign, assign, design, resign, align, benign, malign, diaphragm.

__________ __________ __________ __________

__________ __________ __________ __________

__________ __________ __________ __________

__________

Look up any unfamiliar words in your dictionary. Write the words and their definitions below.

________________________________________

________________________________________

________________________________________

________________________________________

*h* is not sounded in these words:

hour, honor, exhaust, exhibit, vehicle, rhyme, rhythm, rhinoceros, rhubarb, rhapsody, rhetoric, rheumatic, rheumatism, ghost, ghetto, ghoul, ghastly, gherkin, herb.

*k* is not sounded in these words:

knee, know, knowledge, known, knew, knife, knit, knot, knob, knock, knight, kneel, knuckle, knack, knead, knave, knoll, knapsack.

*l* is not sounded in these words:

folk, yolk, balk, talk, walk, chalk, stalk, calf, calves, half, halves.

**Look up any unfamiliar words in your dictionary. Write the words and their definitions below.**

## Silent Letters (continued)

*n* is not sounded in these words:
condemn, hymn, column, autumn, solemn.

*p* is not sounded in these words:
receipt, raspberry, corps, cupboard, pneumonia, pseudonym, psychiatry, psychology.

*s* is not sounded in these words:
isle, island, aisle.

*t* is not sounded in these words:
often, listen, hasten, fasten, moisten, glisten, christen.

*u* is not sounded in these words:
build, built, buy, guess, guest, guide, guard, guilt, guild, guitar, guarantee, guerrilla, plague, rogue, vogue, tongue, league.

*w* is not sounded in these words:

answer, whole, sword, write, written, wrote, wrap, wreath, wreck, wrong, wrist, wrench, wrinkle, wring, wrung, wren, wretched, wrought, wrath, wrangle, wrangler, writhe.

Look up any unfamiliar words in your dictionary. Write the words and their definitions below.

Write five or six original sentences using as many words that contain silent letters as you can.

## Silent Letters (continued)

In the following exercises, write next to each word the letter or letters that are silent in the word.

| *Exercise 1* | | *Exercise 2* | | *Exercise 3* | |
|---|---|---|---|---|---|
| debt | b | wreath | ______ | write | ______ |
| talk | ______ | knit | ______ | knee | ______ |
| hymn | ______ | comb | ______ | numb | ______ |
| sword | ______ | sign | ______ | knot | ______ |
| wrap | ______ | listen | ______ | gnaw | ______ |
| know | ______ | solemn | ______ | column | ______ |
| knife | ______ | scent | ______ | hasten | ______ |
| gnat | ______ | wrong | ______ | ghost | ______ |
| scene | ______ | exhibit | ______ | thumb | ______ |
| rhubarb | ______ | ghastly | ______ | doubt | ______ |
| yolk | ______ | answer | ______ | island | ______ |
| wrote | ______ | walk | ______ | hour | ______ |
| honor | ______ | rhapsody | ______ | often | ______ |
| guard | ______ | wrist | ______ | knew | ______ |
| plumber | ______ | climb | ______ | fasten | ______ |
| lamb | ______ | crumb | ______ | limb | ______ |
| dumb | ______ | guess | ______ | condemn | ______ |
| wrong | ______ | buy | ______ | scissors | ______ |
| whole | ______ | kneel | ______ | bomb | ______ |

**Use a separate sheet of paper to write the sentences dictated by your teacher. This dictation will check your ability to spell words with silent letters.**[1]

[1] Dictate sentences from the list on pages 100, 101, and 102 in *How to Teach Spelling.*

# Sight Word List 5

Read and copy these words. Learn to spell them.

| | | | |
|---|---|---|---|
| senior | ______ | February | ______ |
| straight | ______ | Wednesday | ______ |
| calm | ______ | Fahrenheit | ______ |
| palm | ______ | Celsius | ______ |
| ache | ______ | imagine | ______ |
| iron | ______ | engine | ______ |
| onion | ______ | medicine | ______ |
| salad | ______ | disease | ______ |
| aisle | ______ | vacuum | ______ |
| isle | ______ | squirrel | ______ |
| island | ______ | mosquito | ______ |
| juice | ______ | restaurant | ______ |
| fruit | ______ | library | ______ |
| suit | ______ | guarantee | ______ |
| cruise | ______ | cordial | ______ |
| bruise | ______ | cereal | ______ |
| biscuit | ______ | recipe | ______ |
| terrible | ______ | yacht | ______ |
| anxious | ______ | scissors | ______ |
| necessary | ______ | soldier | ______ |
| cousin | ______ | sergeant | ______ |
| aunt | ______ | lieutenant | ______ |
| America | ______ | colonel | ______ |
| century | ______ | bureau | ______ |

## Sight Word List 5 (continued)

| | | | |
|---|---|---|---|
| million | ________________ | spaghetti | ________________ |
| billion | ________________ | chocolate | ________________ |
| bullion | ________________ | nuisance | ________________ |
| bouillon | ________________ | capitol (building) | ________________ |

**After you know how to spell all the words on Sight Word List 5, use a separate sheet of paper to write the sentences dictated by your teacher.**[1]

[1] Dictate sentences from the list on pages 103 and 104 in *How to Teach Spelling*.